RESEARCH TOOL KIT

PRESENT WHAT YOU KNOW

Sharing Information

by Christopher Forest

Consultant:
Gwen Hart, PhD
Assistant Professor of English Composition
Buena Vista University
Storm Lake, Iowa

CAPSTONE PRESS
a capstone imprint

Fact Finders are published by Capstone Press,
1710 Roe Crest Drive, North Mankato, Minnesota 56003
www.capstonepub.com

Library of Congress Cataloging-in-Publication Data
Forest, Christopher.
Present what you know : sharing information / by Christopher Forest.
    pages cm. — (Fact finders. Research tool kit)
Summary: "Explores ways to share information when doing research and writing reports
and other written materials"—Provided by publisher.
Includes bibliographical references and index.
  ISBN 978-1-4296-9949-5 (library binding)
  ISBN 978-1-62065-788-1 (paperback)
  ISBN 978-1-4765-1569-4 (ebook PDF)
 1. Report writing—Juvenile literature. 2. Composition (Language arts)—Juvenile literature.
3. Research—Juvenile literature. I. Title.
  LB1047.3.F67 2013
  372.62'3—dc23
                              2012029368

Editorial Credits
Kristen Mohn, editor; Juliette Peters, designer; Eric Manske, production specialist

Photo Credits
Alamy: Kuttig — People, 22; Capstone Studio: Karon Dubke, 11 (left), 20, 24, 27 (bottom),
29; Corbis: Bettmann, 16 (protesters), 18 (inset), ClassicStock/H. Armstrong Roberts, 16
(families, dancer), Rick Friedman, 15; Courtesy of www.prezi.com, 17; Newscom: Altopress/
Eric Audras, 28; Shutterstock: Alexander Raths, 8, auremar, 18, blue67design, cover (phone),
DM7, 13 (bottom), Gertjan Hooijer, 26, iodrakon, 4, Jan Kaliciak, 13 (top, both), Johan
Swanepoel, 11 (right), Lagartija de colores, 27 (top), MisterElements, cover (light bulb), 9,
Ronald Sumners, 7 (top), schwarzhana, 7 (bottom), Tischenko Irina, 6; Wikimedia: NARA/
Cecil Stoughton, White House, 16 (JFK)

Artistic Effects
Shutterstock: Erica Truex, MisterElements

Printed in the United States of America in North Mankato, Minnesota.
102013   007757R

TABLE OF CONTENTS

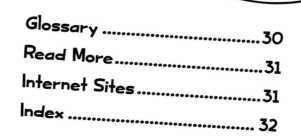

Spread the Word!

You've got a report to write or a presentation to prepare. Or maybe you've got an opinion, a message, or a bit of great knowledge you want to share—with your friends, or with the world!

So How to Go about It?

First think about the medium you want to use. That means the format you'll present your information in. It could be anything from a written report to a poster or even a speech you make over the loudspeaker in the cafeteria!

What does the assignment call for? What format would work best for the type of information you want to share? Who is your audience? After all, you would present a message differently to your Scout troop than you would to a preschool class. Those are all things to think about as you prepare to present what you know.

HERE ARE JUST A FEW OF THE WAYS YOU CAN SHARE INFORMATION:

speech · video · blog · instructions · diagram · pamphlet · poster · timeline · review · advertisement · script · website · board game · graph · report · poem · word cloud · slideshow · news report · essay · chart · journal · biography · brochure · commercial · collage · map · book trailer · podcast · editorial · illustration · puppet show · newsletter · cartoon strip · dialogue · diorama · skit · song

audience—the people you want to hear your message

5

Research Writing

Writing is one of the most effective ways to share what you know. People have been using "words" to get the word out for thousands of years! Writing to provide information is called expository writing.

Written language was invented around 3200 BC in Mesopotamia—modern-day Iraq.

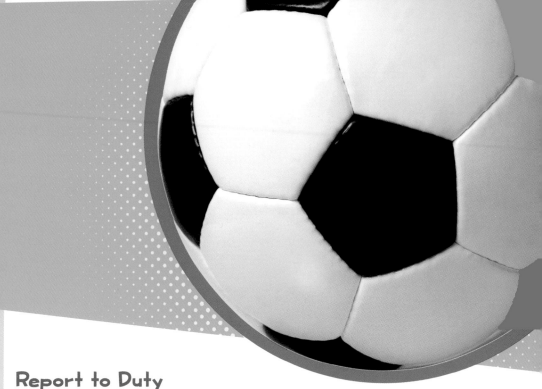

Report to Duty

Suppose you want to tell everything you've learned about soccer, or the life story of your grandfather, who fought in the Vietnam War. A great way to share a lot of research about something is by writing a report.

Steps to Success:

STEP 1

Decide on a topic. If you have a choice, make it something that interests you. That way the experience is more fun. If your teacher insists that you write about the history of broccoli, put a fun spin on it. You could write as if you were a piece of broccoli talking about your family history!

STEP 2

Research. Find facts about your topic. Use reliable sources, such as encyclopedias, **nonfiction** books or magazines, and official websites. A librarian can help you determine the best sources to use. You may also use first-person sources. These are people, such as scientists or historians, who are experts on particular topics. Or they may have experienced an event you are writing about.

STEP 3

Develop a thesis. A thesis is a statement that explains what you'll be writing about. It's best to have a specific thesis. For instance, instead of just writing about soccer, consider focusing on one aspect of the sport, such as "Soccer requires five essential skills." That way you can go into more detail.

STEP 4

Make a plan. Organize your thoughts into three parts. The first part is an introduction that tells about the thesis. Then comes the body of the report. This should contain strong word choices to keep your reader interested. Finally, add a conclusion to summarize what you've covered.

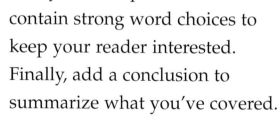

nonfiction—writing that's factual

8

WHEN TRYING TO GATHER INFORMATION, MOST STUDENTS RACE TO THE INTERNET.

BUT WATCH OUT!

Some websites are made by non-experts. Ask yourself:

- Who created the website and why?
- When was it last updated?
- What is the purpose of the website?

If the website is designed to make money, the information may not be 100 percent accurate. Official sites run by not-for-profit organizations, educational institutions, or the government are often the most reliable. Check out sites ending in .org or .edu or .gov.

Go Worldwide with a Website

Websites are pages on the Internet that contain information. The best sites often are ones that share information about a specific topic, such as the "10 best paper airplane designs" or "flags of the world," rather than general topics, such as "sports." You can use the Internet to share your information by building your own website. A website is an especially good medium to use to share your information if you've got video, audio, or other elements to include.

Tips:

- Any information you **post** needs to be current and accurate.
- Use reliable sources to find your facts.
- List the sources you used on your site so that visitors can check them and see that you aren't just making stuff up.

Several websites help students develop their own safe websites. Ask a teacher or librarian for help. Also ask if your school has a secure server. A secure sever allows you to design a site just for the students in your school.

post—to publish writing on the Internet

AVOIDING PLAGIARISM

When researching, you sometimes come across a great idea or statement another person had. But be careful! You always have to state whose idea it is.

In a report on giraffes, you might write that giraffes aren't always gentle giants:

According to Jack Hanna of the Columbus Zoo and Aquarium, Masai giraffes can use their hooves to "inflict serious injury."

Don't just copy the idea word for word or summarize it like it's yours. Use quotations for direct quotes, and always include the source. Otherwise it's plagiarism, a type of stealing.

Get Noticed with Newsletters

Do you have local news you want to share? Is something amazing happening at your school? Newsletters are a simple way to get your information out to a specific audience. They can be shared online, or you can print copies to give to people.

A newsletter looks like a mini newspaper. It is typically a two-sided page that resembles the front and back of a newspaper page. It's filled with notes, small articles, pictures, and facts on subjects that relate to one another. A school newsletter includes topics that relate to the school.

Newsletters are good choices if you want to share a collection of brief reports that all relate to a theme. If you're interested in Mars, your newsletter might contain sections such as "Mars Weather," "Mars Facts," and "Are There Really Martians?"

Steps to Success:

STEP 1 Write several sections, each about five to seven sentences long.

STEP 2 Include lots of pictures, quotes, charts, and graphs to show information.

STEP 3 Don't forget small text boxes that feature short snippets of information.

MARS

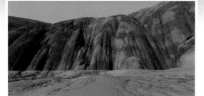

Mars Facts

_____
_____
_____
_____

Mars Weather

_____
_____
_____
_____

Are There Really Martians?

" _____
_____
_____ "
_____
_____
_____

Newsletter Help

Many word processing programs have templates that will help you make newsletters. Pictures and other visuals may be added with a simple click.

CHAPTER TWO

Presentation Writing

Most writing is meant to be read. Sometimes a message is meant to be heard. In a presentation you can share your information in person. There's still writing involved in a presentation, but you can let your voice do the talking.

Speeches: In the Spotlight

The next time you watch the president on TV, pay careful attention. The president is probably reading a speech. Professionals make giving a speech look as easy as talking. But a successful speech needs more than just a mouth.

Steps to Success:

 STEP 1 Determine two or three main points that you want to share.

 STEP 2 Start with something attention-grabbing to hook your listener. It might be a little-known fact or a startling story. Use lively language to keep your audience listening.

 STEP 3 Make eye contact with your audience and use gestures to emphasize points. Avoid speaking in one tone. Put enthusiasm into your voice.

STEP 4
At the end of your speech, remind the audience of your key ideas. End on a note that will keep them thinking about what you said.

STEP 5
Practice! Give your speech in front of a mirror first, and then in front of a friend, parent, or other adult. They might have questions or suggestions you can use to improve your speech.

Speechmakers often write speeches on note cards to help jog their memory as they're speaking. If you use cards, don't write out your entire speech—just write down the main points you want to remember. Instead of reading, look at your notes, then use your own words to explain them. That will make your speech sound fresh. It will also be easier for you to look at your audience to keep them engaged.

How-To Speeches

Any topic can work for a speech, but demonstrations work especially well. You might teach an audience how the banana-peeling machine you invented works. Or you might demonstrate the steps involved in juggling.

Share Your Speech with a Slideshow

Sometimes you might want to take a speech to the next level. Maybe you want to show a desert ecosystem. Or perhaps you want to show what life was like in the 1960s when your grandma was a go-go dancer. Combine technology and writing to make a show-stopping slideshow.

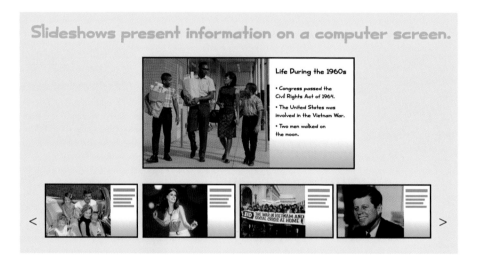

Slideshows present information on a computer screen.

Slideshow presenters design screens (the slides) with ideas that support their topic. Most slides contain information in bullets, which are brief statements, and a picture or photo with a caption.

The presenter usually guides the slideshow, giving extra information about each slide. This presentation takes the form of a speech. Most slideshow programs have an option to see a "presenter's view," so you can see your notes on your screen as well as what your audience is seeing.

caption—information about a picture or photograph

Have just one or two main ideas on each screen.

 Use the same background throughout. It makes your message stick together.

 Type with a font size between 18 and 22 so it's easy for the audience to see.

 Don't overdo pictures, colors, animations, or sounds. It could distract from the information you're trying to share.

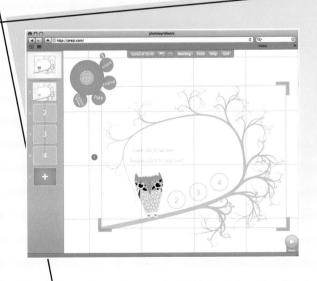

Where to Begin?

Several programs and websites can help students make slideshows. These include PowerPoint, Keynote, Animoto, Prezi, Google Documents, and many others. Ask your teacher or librarian for help.

Giving Directions

We hear directions every day. Whether we're asking how to get to the park or how to play a game, we need directions. Have you ever been confused after hearing or reading directions? That's because giving them is not as easy as it sounds! Writing or presenting directions is an art form that you can master.

Directions list the steps needed to do a task. Before writing directions:

- Make sure you understand all of the steps.
- Think about how you can explain the steps in the clearest way possible.
- Test your directions on someone to see how easy they are to follow.

Julia Child was a famous chef who demonstrated her cooking on TV shows in the '60s, '70s, and '80s.

Steps to Success:

STEP 1 Make all of your steps simple and clear. Use specific language to help your audience picture each part or step.

STEP 2 Don't give too much information at once. For instance, if you are giving the steps for tying a shoe, you can't talk about loops, knots, and twirls all in one step. Each motion should be one step in the directions.

STEP 3 Don't assume your audience knows things that you know, such as cooking terms if you're sharing a recipe.

STEP 4 Use transition words to order or connect ideas and information. These are words or phrases such as also, because, first, for example, or finally. They help the reader or audience link one idea to another.

PODCASTS: INFORMATION THAT LASTS

Sometimes you have a message you want to share that will need to be repeated. Perhaps a listener was not at your presentation. Maybe you are sharing how to tie a fishing knot—people will need to hear the steps again once they find their fishing line. A podcast is an audio or video recording of your presentation. You can post your podcast online. The best part is, listeners can go to your podcast any time they want.

CHAPTER THREE

Persuasive Writing

Do you have an opinion you just have to share? Do you want other people to see your position or point-of-view? Writing persuasively will get your point across.

Sway Them with an Essay

A persuasive essay is a writing piece that expresses an opinion you feel strongly about. Maybe it's how your community can help those in need, or why you should have less homework. A persuasive essay lets people know your thoughts and ideas. And, you hope, it will convince them to agree with you.

Steps to Success:

STEP 1

State your claim. This is your opinion or belief that you want others to hear. Your claim should be easy to understand.

STEP 2

Provide reasons. Find at least three strong reasons to support your opinion. Then think carefully about how you want to arrange them. Perhaps you want to start off with your best reason. Or you might prefer to save your best reason for last.

STEP 3

Give supporting facts and evidence from your research. For example, if you want to defend why students should have less homework, talk about the scientific study you found that stated homework adds to student stress. Or perhaps you found research stating that too much homework keeps students from getting enough exercise. Include those facts to help support your position.

STEP 4

End strong. The conclusion is the last part of your essay. Now that you've made your points, tell the readers what to do with the information. What steps can they take to further the cause?

Whose Idea Was It?

When writing a persuasive essay, you might want to share points that another person made. Make sure to give proper credit to that person. It will reinforce your opinion and make it known that others share it.

Sell It with a Script

Has a commercial ever convinced you to buy something? Have you ever seen a movie trailer and knew you just had to see that movie? If so, then you have been sold by a script.

Scripts, also known as commercials, allow you to show your opinion as well as tell it. And they're fun to perform! But before you start acting, you'll need to prepare your script.

- Identify characters and narrators.
- Include expressions and actions for characters to perform.
- Provide lines of **dialogue** for the characters to say. The dialogue provides reasons why the audience should agree with your opinion.

dialogue—the speaking parts of characters

Speaker One: (speaking excitedly, holding up new phone) Check out my new cell phone! My parents finally let me get one!

Speaker Two: (looking discouraged) No fair! I've been asking my parents for one for years, but they still say no!

Speaker One: Ask them to get you the new BrainFone! All you have to do is answer two math questions before every call. It's easy!

Narrator: (in a salesperson's voice) The new BrainFone is a great way to keep in touch with your kids AND make sure they've done their homework!

HUMOR ALWAYS HELPS

Sometimes the easiest way to make a point is to use humor. In a cartoon or comic strip, you can make your point with clever words and pictures. Newspapers and magazines use these types of cartoons every day. Often the cartoon exaggerates something happening in current events. These cartoons are called political cartoons. They're quick, eye-catching ways to state an opinion.

CHAPTER FOUR

Narrative Writing

Do you have an interesting life story? Have you had an interesting or unusual experience that you want to share? Narrative nonfiction writing is a type of writing that tells a story.

Journaling: A Writing Journey

A journal is a first-person account of daily events. You may keep a journal for yourself. Or you may write a public journal that's meant to be read by others.

You might journal—write in a journal—to record what happens each day at school. Or you might journal about your summer adventures. Some people keep nature journals to record the animals they've seen. Teachers might assign book journals for you to write about the books you've read. You can journal about anything you like!

Writing a journal is a cinch. All you need is a notebook or an online journal to track events. Besides what you write, you can add other things to a journal. You may put in small items, such as movie tickets, pamphlets from a museum you visited, or sketches of a bird you saw.

FAMOUS JOURNALS

Your journal may be a primary source some day. This means that historians can use it to learn from people who lived in our times. Famous journals have told us a lot about the past. Leonardo da Vinci's journal tells about inventions from centuries ago. Laura Ingalls Wilder turned her journal-style writing into The Little House Books series. They share a first-person account of her life in pioneer times.

Post It with a Blog

You might have a topic that you want to update your audience on daily or weekly. For example, you might want to write about how your baby sister is changing each day. Or maybe you want to share progress on a science project about moldy cheese. A blog is the perfect way to make people aware of new and changing information.

Blogs are daily logs kept on a website that allow you to talk about topics that interest you. Like journals, blogs share first-hand information. Visitors from all over the world can visit your blog. They can read your posts, see pictures, watch videos, and even respond to you.

Once you get good at blogging, you might try creating a vlog—a video blog. It is a video that shares your story. Some people even turn their vlogs into regular Internet TV shows.

log—a written record

Privacy, Please!

Never post personal information online that reveals your identity. Do not include your last name, address, or other details that you wouldn't want strangers to know.

BIG BROTHER blog

Josie Laughed!
September 8

Today my sister laughed for the first time. Mom said it was probably not a real laugh—she said it was gas! But I'm sure I made her laugh. Josie thinks I'm funny!

World's Fastest Eater
September 5

Today my parents let me feed Josie. It was so much fun!!! She drank her whole bottle in less than three minutes. Then I had to learn how to burp her, which was not as much fun. She spit up on me!

Recent Posts

Diapers, Diapers!

Crying All Night

Cutest Baby Ever

Meet Baby Josie!

Blog Archive

2012 (6)

August (3)

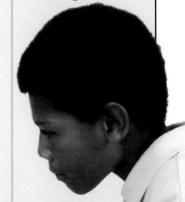

27

Your Audience Awaits ...

There are nearly as many ways to present your information as there are topics to present! Think about what your goals are—are you trying to inform people? Convince them? Warn them? Entertain them? Who do you want to hear your message? Knowing these things can help you decide the best format to use.

Keep in mind that you can use any style of writing—expository, persuasive, or narrative—in any medium. For instance, you might decide to create a persuasive website about why rats are great pets. Or your slideshow might be a narrative story of your experience at summer camp. You can use whatever style of writing that works best for your goal.

Most important, have fun and be creative! Professional writers are always looking for new and interesting ways to catch people's attention. Whether it's a walking billboard or a speech written in rhyme, there are hundreds of ways to get your message out!

GLOSSARY

audience (AW-dee-uhns)—people who read or listen to a presentation

caption (CAP-shun)—the information that appears with a photo or image

dialogue (DY-uh-lawg)—the words spoken between two or more characters

first-person (FURST PER-suhn)—coming from a person who directly experienced something or who has personal knowledge on a subject

log (LAWG)—a written record

nonfiction (NON-fik-shuhn)—written work about real people, places, objects, or events

plagiarism (PLAY-jer-ihz-um)—copying someone else's work and passing it off as your own

political cartoon (puh-LIT-uh-kuhl car-TOON)—a cartoon that uses humor to make a point or share an idea

post (POHST)—to print or publish something for others to read, particularly on the Internet

thesis (THEE-sis)—a statement, opinion, or topic of writing

visitor (VIH-zih-tur)—a person who views a website

vlog (VLAWG)—a video blog

READ MORE

Bentley, Nancy. *Don't Be a Copycat!: Write a Great Report without Plagiarizing.* Berkeley Heights, N.J.: Enslow Elementary, 2008.

Fandel, Jennifer. *Picture Yourself Writing Nonfiction: Using Photos to Inspire Writing.* See It. Write It. Mankato, Minn.: Capstone Press, 2012.

Gaines, Ann Graham. *Ace Your Research Paper.* Ace It! Information Literacy Series. Berkeley Heights, N.J.: Enslow Elementary, 2009.

Rosinsky, Natalie M. *Write Your Own Nonfiction.* Write Your Own. Minneapolis: Compass Point Books, 2009.

Somervill, Barbara A. *Written Reports.* School Projects Survival Guides. Chicago: Heinemann Library, 2009.

INTERNET SITES

FactHound offers a safe, fun way to find Internet sites related to this book. All of the sites on FactHound have been researched by our staff.

Here's all you do:

Visit *www.facthound.com*

Type in this code: 9781429699495

Check out projects, games and lots more at
www.capstonekids.com

INDEX